Let Us Bring Order

Workbook

Verleiz Lattimore, MBA, MED

Copyright © 2013 Verleiz Lattimore

All rights reserved.

ISBN: 0988263246
ISBN-13: 978-0-9882632-4-6

DEDICATION

Dedicated To Alvin Lattimore

Only You!

Table Of Contents

Introduction	3
Whose Life is This?	5
See Yourself Whole, See Yourself Rich	28
Delete the Negatives	35
Handling and Circulating Your Money	49
Your Own Boss	72
Why Four Streams	82
Money Matters	95
Taste the Success	104
Mediation – Relaxation	125
Mentors and Mentorship	135
Becoming A Mentor	143
New Beginnings	151

ACKNOWLEDGMENTS

Thanks to my mom who is still leading and guiding, you will always be my number one hero.

To my husband, my Alvin, thanks for the support and help, love you to life.

To my Morgan, Tee- Tee does it all to see you do better.

Also my big brother, thanks for believing in me even when you didn't see the plan.

Purpose for this workbook

This book has been designed to help you take the principles and keys from the *Let Us Begin Order* text to get the maximum results. As you navigate these pages you will begin to find the answers from within that will allow you to grow and evolve your dreams. I can give you the keys but it is up to you to use them. That is why this workbook is so important. It will allow you to make the steps on your time and in a fashion that will put things in the best light for you.

Your success is driven by your decisions and the honesty that you use to deal with life. No one will judge you in this process but you, as you are the creator of your own change. Know that at times you may have to take time with your answers and decisions but that is what this is all about. You are making the decisions that will give you the freedom to unlock your hidden potential and ultimately your success.

Each exercise is a guide to the focus needed to understand where to address change so that you are not stumbling blindly through the change process that will begin as you read the *Let Us Bring Order* text and access where you are and where you need to be. This is just the beginning of your journey but this workbook will help to guide you on the path of a great transform. In addition, you will find more assistance at www.LetUsBringOrder.com and www.RennyConsulting.com.

The author Verleiz will talk you through the chapters and exercises in this workbook and you will know that you are not alone in this new beginning but moving along with great encouragement. Everyone will experience this workbook differently but all will be glad for the experience as it will add to you and those around you. Enjoy the next steps to your success.

~Introduction~

What goes up has once been down; we should never fear failure because it is only feedback. It is not who you are when you arrive it is what you do when you are on the journey. Success is in the process of creating the success and being willing to take the risks.

Many people never get passed the idea because they never make the first step. Fear of the first step paralyzes individuals into failure. How can you know what you are capable of if you don't try? You have thankfully made a first step by purchasing this book. Congratulations! You get in life what you invest in and you are a great investment. All you need is to invest your thoughts into your true potential and success.

I believe I can help you met your goals because I have come to understand the model of success. I have come to a place in life were success is magnetized to me the same way I know I can show you to magnetize success to you. I believe in your ability to change your life into the one you have imagined therefore I want to give you the keys I know will insure you the success you desire. I know that reading this book will be an eye opener for you and after you do so you will begin to feel the world open up to you. If I can share but one secret to success with you while we take this journey together I can offer you the keys to freeing your mind to accomplish anything your heart desires. I can assure you this book will renew your mind as I offer you these tested truths, so that I can do as life does and give to the giver.

I want to take this journey with you because I believe in sharing what I have learned. At the age of thirty-one I find that just the right information and the right amount of risk can help you to move forward. I took a risk when I went to college for Fashion Design and acquired an Associate's Degree. I took another risk when I went on to get my Bachelor's in Education and Psychology. I turned around and took yet three more risks when I went from my MBA in Marketing and Project Management, to my MED in Curriculum Design and Instructional Technology and then another Bachelor's in Metaphysics. All of these risks paid off in the end because they gave me specialized knowledge that has help to build my businesses and ideas. It may not make sense to some but all my risks make sense to my plans and goals.

I found what I loved in life and pursued a means to make it all work together for my success. You too can find what it is you want from life the most and make great things happen for you. It is not about what the world labels you as; it is what you will label yourself as. You have the God given right to create a great life for you and your family.

In these pages you will find your road map to success on your own terms. You will make the links with what will catapult you into your greatest potential. Life is like clay you have to mold the experience you desire. You want change you have to create it, and you are more than able to do so.

This book will help you to once again find your voice, as you begin to feel alive and in control again. You will see yourself for the great, successful person you are. Let's begin this journey to the new you together. I want you to decide now whether you are truly ready for change. Do you know you want better? Are you ready to find out how to get better? Are you ready to be set free? If you have said yes to all of these questions I want you to begin to make a promise to yourself. Write in the space belong, **YES I CAN!!!!!** And sign your name.

(Signed here for your success)

You have just promised yourself success. We shall find the hidden treasure within you. Let Us Bring Order!

~Who's Life is This?~

Chapter One

One of the first steps to moving forward in your life is to ask yourself, *who's life is this?* Are you living the life you want or a life planned by someone else? When you look in the mirror of your life are you seeing something or someone you like? Many of us wander the earth for years following the blueprint that someone else has drawn, never fulfilling the actions that are in the blueprints that are given to us for our own dreams. Hearing the voice of another and not listening to the voice of our own experience.

So once again I ask, *who's life is this?* Are you living the life you want or living the life that someone has planned for you? Most likely without even knowing it you are living the life someone else has planned for you, however by now you have realized you are ready to live the life planned by you. So first, it is time for you to sit down and find out what is in this plan of yours.

Exercise #1

The reason planning is so important is that it literally directs your path, without a vision the people parish. If you feel like you are vanishing, then you have failed to focus in on the vision for your life. Goals are the key, so let's start with forming your goals.

I always advise my clients to start by listing ten goals. These are the goals that line up your plan; they are the foundation of your blueprint. You need to make these goals solid and treat them as anchors for your life. You should also be mindful of the goals you are setting because these are truly those things that will carry you to the next level. So list things that hold meaning and truly hold your hearts desires.

> **WHO DO YOU WANT TO BE IN LIFE? WHAT DO YOU WANT TO SEE MANIFEST? WHAT IS IT YOU FEEL YOU WANT TO ACCOMPLISH? WHAT IS YOUR INNER VOICE SAYING TO YOU?**

Many individuals want the new home, the husband or wife, or the successful financial life. These are goals that will motive positive outcomes. Change comes through and from motivation. What will motive you? What goals will cause you to get in gear and really work at the increase in your happiness? These are the goals you start with no matter how large they are, the bigger the dream the more motivation. You see greatness is waiting dormant in you, waiting for you to plan for it to come out. It is not waiting for your best friend to say it is there or for your parents to give it direction. ***It is waiting for you!*** You have to live your own life, you have to give yourself permission to move in the things that life has for you.

> ***How to Do This Exercise:*** In the chart provided list five personal goals you wish to accomplish in the next 6 months to a year. Then list five business goals you wish to accomplish in the next 6 months to a year. ***Ex:*** <u>Personal Goal</u> - *Buy a Home* / <u>Business Goal</u> – *Write my first book.* The point is to list goals that you can move toward and plan around to successfully complete. Remember this is about you and your successful journey to happiness.

Personal Goal	Time Frame	Business Goal	Time Frame
Ex: Debt Cancellation	*Ex: 5 months*	*Ex: Start a New Website*	*Ex:12 months*
1.		1.	
2.		2.	
3.		3.	
4.		4.	
5.		5.	

Exercise #2

Why limit yourself? Tap into those goals that take you into your dreams. If you are working in an office right now in your dream occupation and you have two supervisors above you, make it your business to see yourself in the top position. That should be your goal. No matter if you are not educated enough or if you are not outgoing enough. These are things you can change, and these things change by first setting the goals to change them. The larger the goals the more you can change.

How to Do This Exercise: *Let's evaluate where you are and where you want to be.* This will show us what steps you need to take to get to your goal. Find your place on the steps to success, be honest with yourself. The top of the steps is your goal fulfilled the bottom is the goal not started yet. Locate your position and we will have a starting point, then we can begin to fill in the blanks. You want to do this for all ten of your goals.

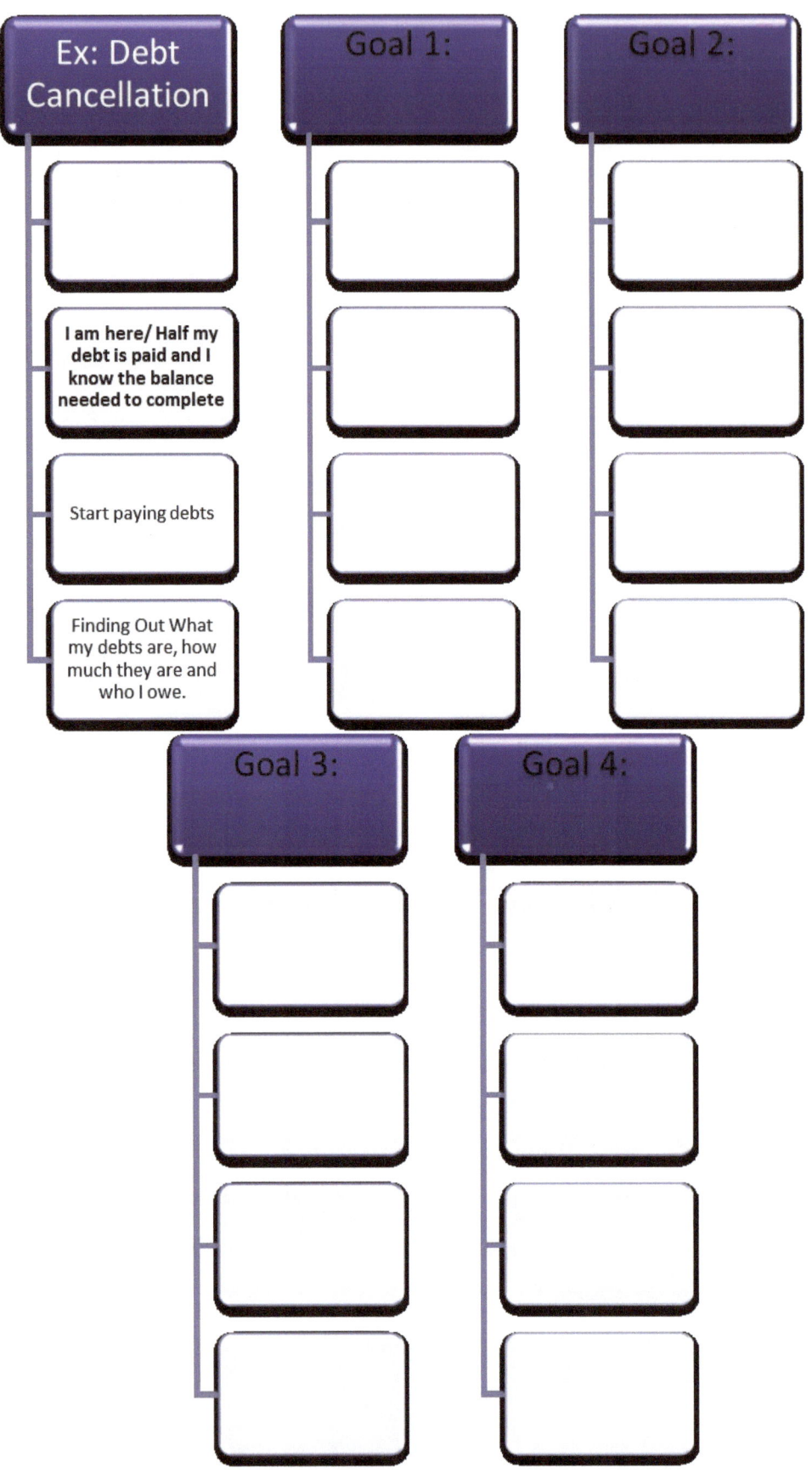

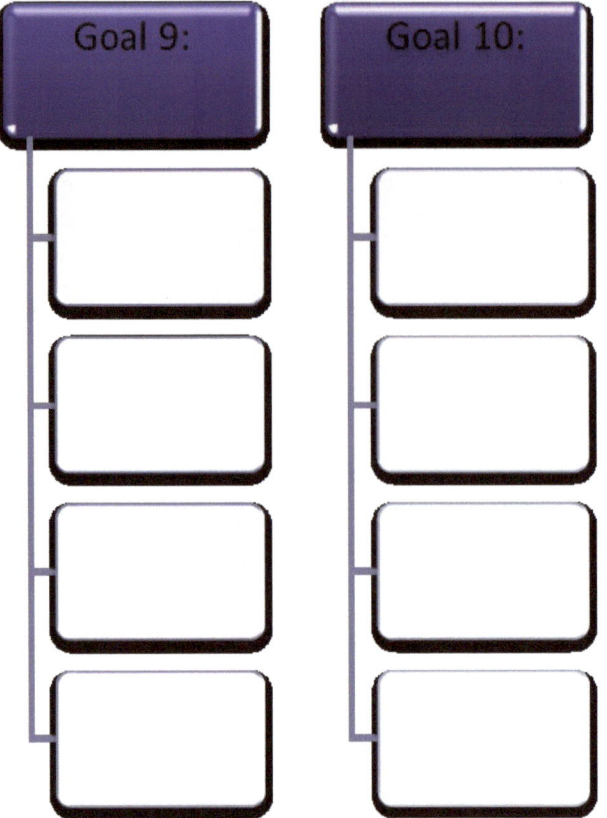

Exercise # 3

Many of us fear change. Let me first state that fear is totally useless. Fear will kill the dream, the vision and the goals. Face your fear first! The best way to face fear is by saying to yourself, "this is my life, and I am not going to take it anymore." Then take the first action that will lead you to the goal you desire. Success takes willingness and the ability to take risks. Taking action puts you in the state of believing you can do. You have now stepped around fear into the position to decide that you are going to hold the vision you have your heart set on.

Facing your fears gives you a sense of receiving your power back. You gain the feeling of the restoration of the energy you were letting go of by conceding to those fears. This is your time to take back your power now!

> ***How to Do This Exercise:*** *Face your fears.* What is holding you back from your goal? What are you afraid of? If you can list the fears you can face them. You will also see that you can eliminate them. Trace your palm on a sheet of paper and write your fears on the inside of the palm. When you are done place your hand under the palm and crumple the page. Your fears are just that easy to crush!!

Exercise #4

Resources are important to your goals and accomplishing the things you envision for you. The more resources the more you can count on making it to the goal. Anything can begin to lend itself as a resource; a relationship, finances, connections, or technology.

> ***How to Do This Exercise:*** *Resources are the Key.* You need resources to make steps so let's evaluate your resources. This will help to figure out what you have and don't have. This way you are aware of your strengths and your areas where growth and development are needed. List the resources you have to accomplish each goal you have set. In the space provided enter your goal and then begin to fill in your resources.

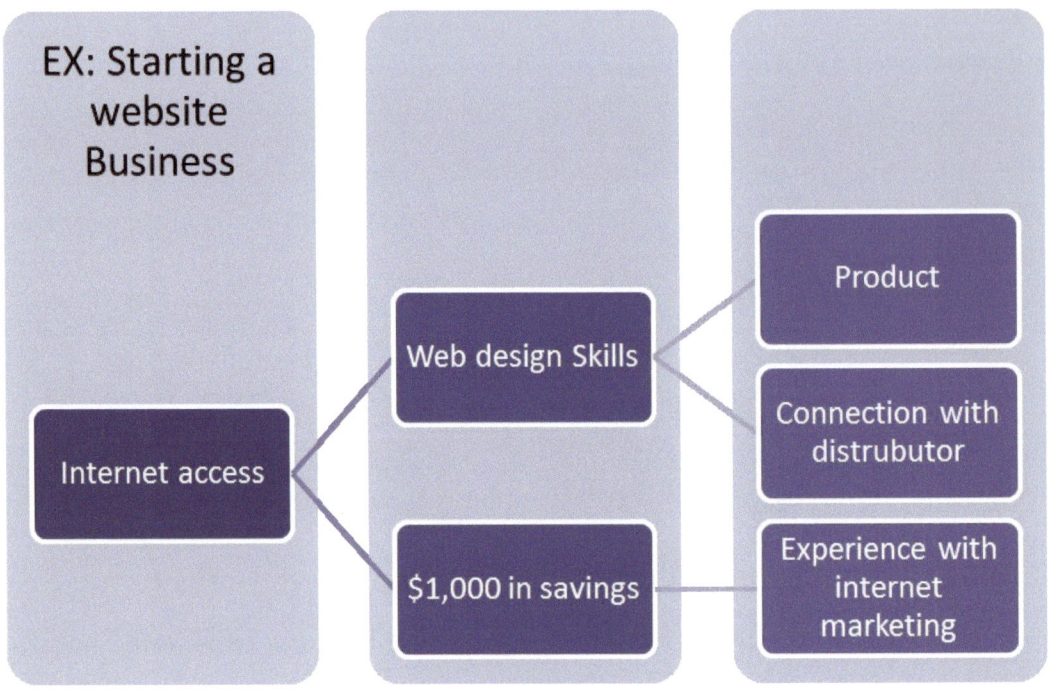

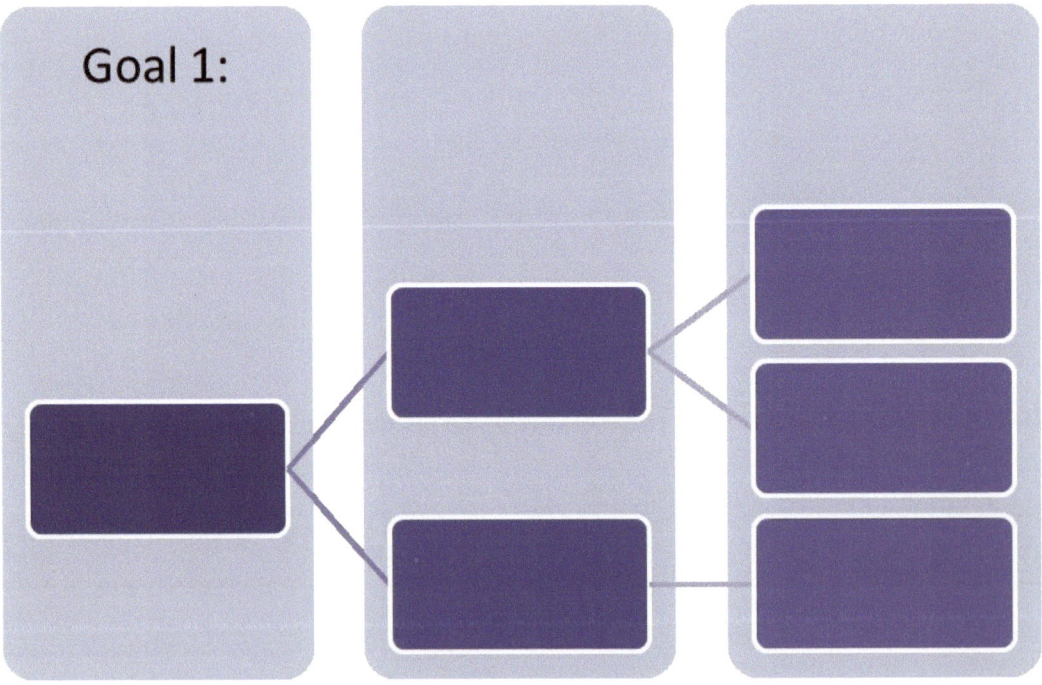

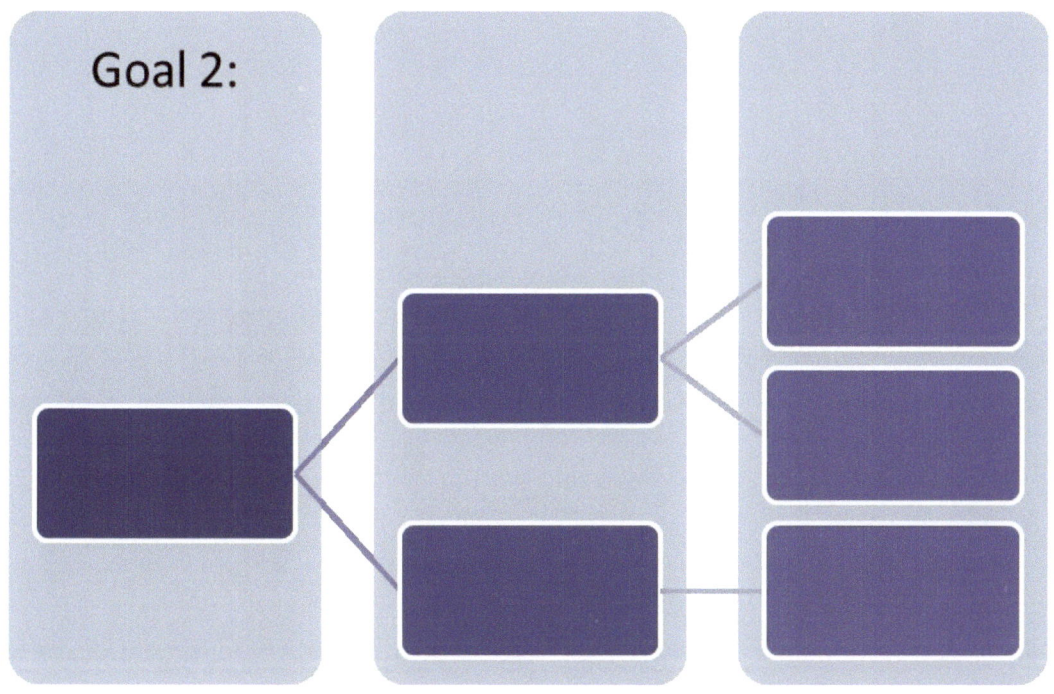
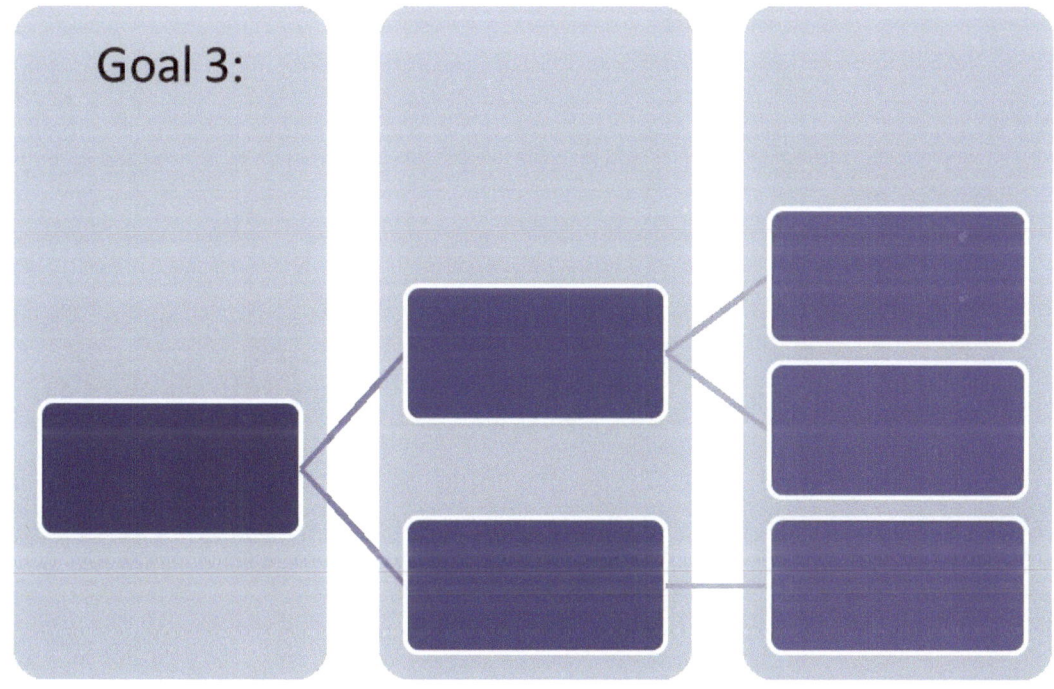

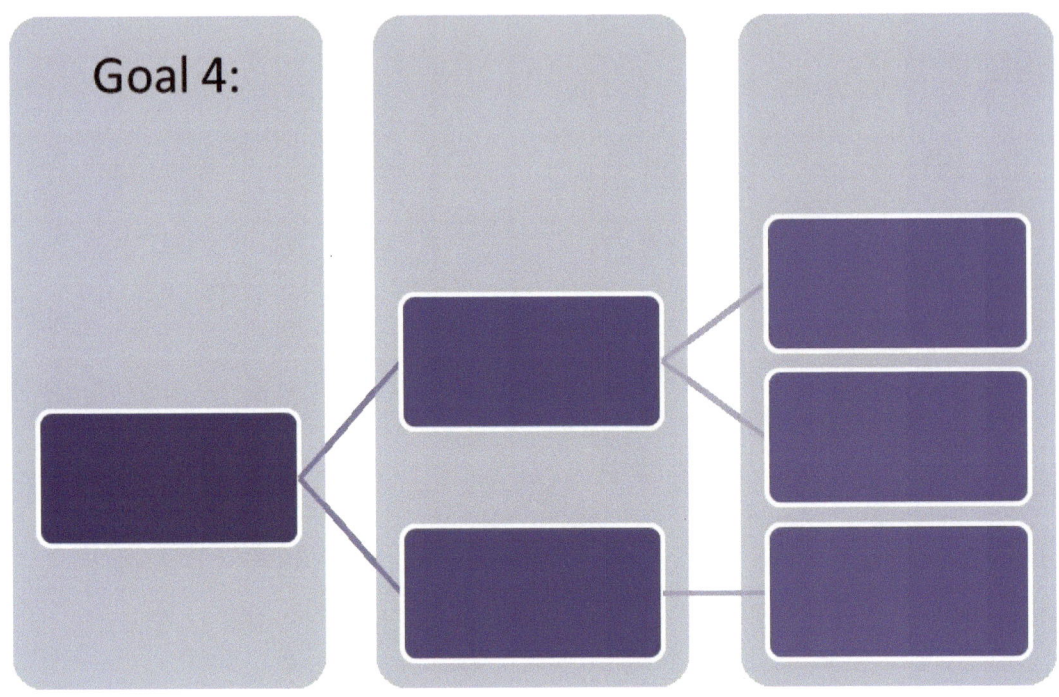
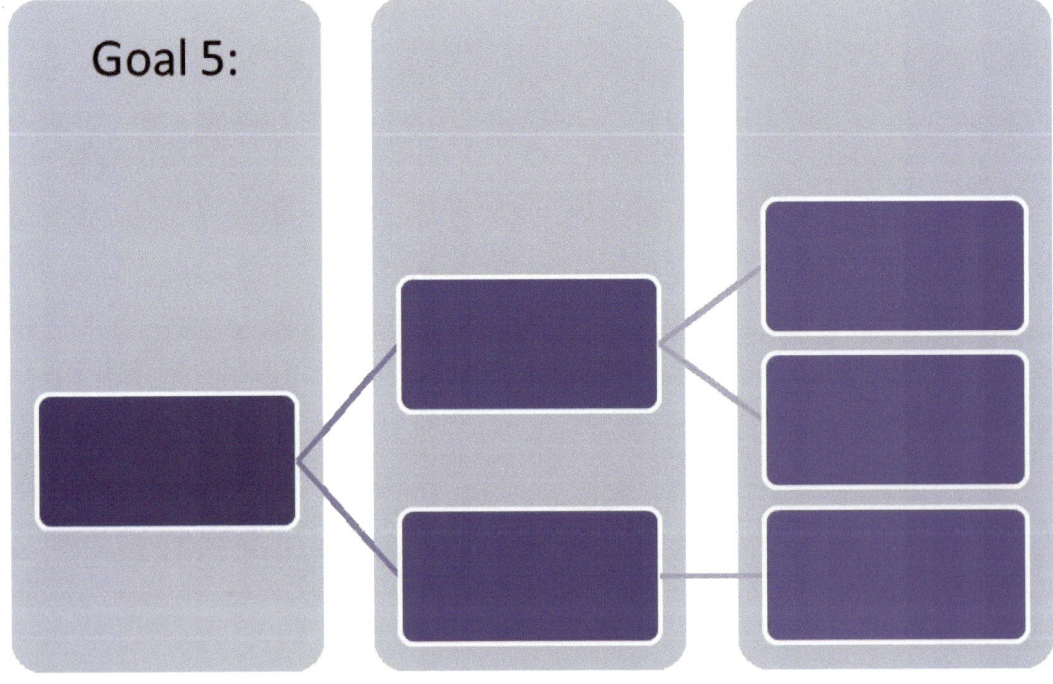

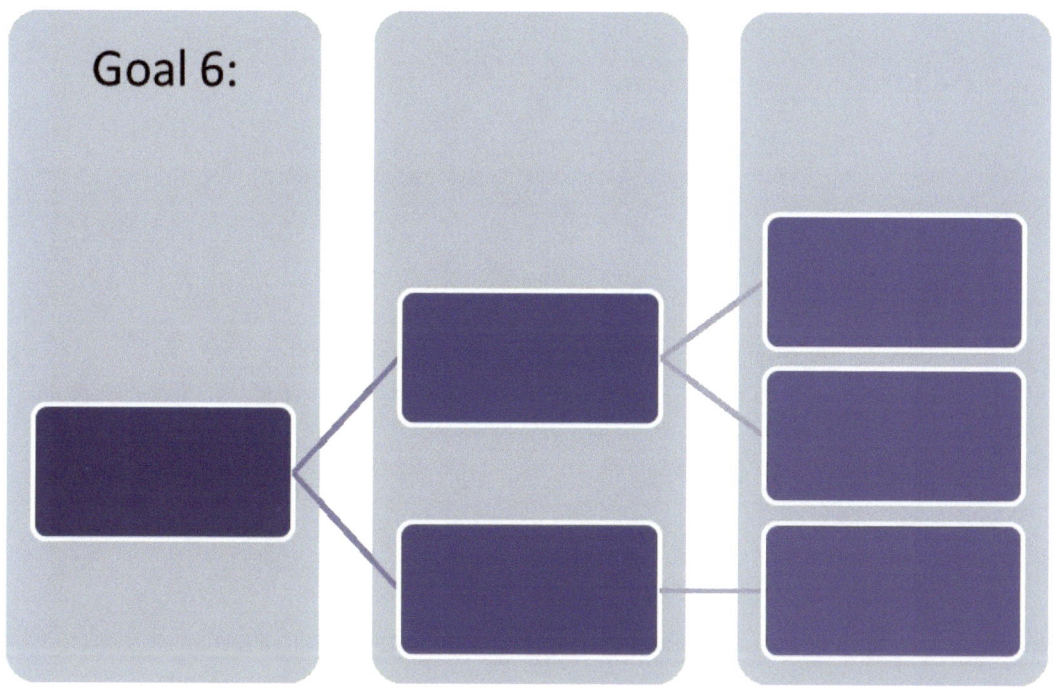

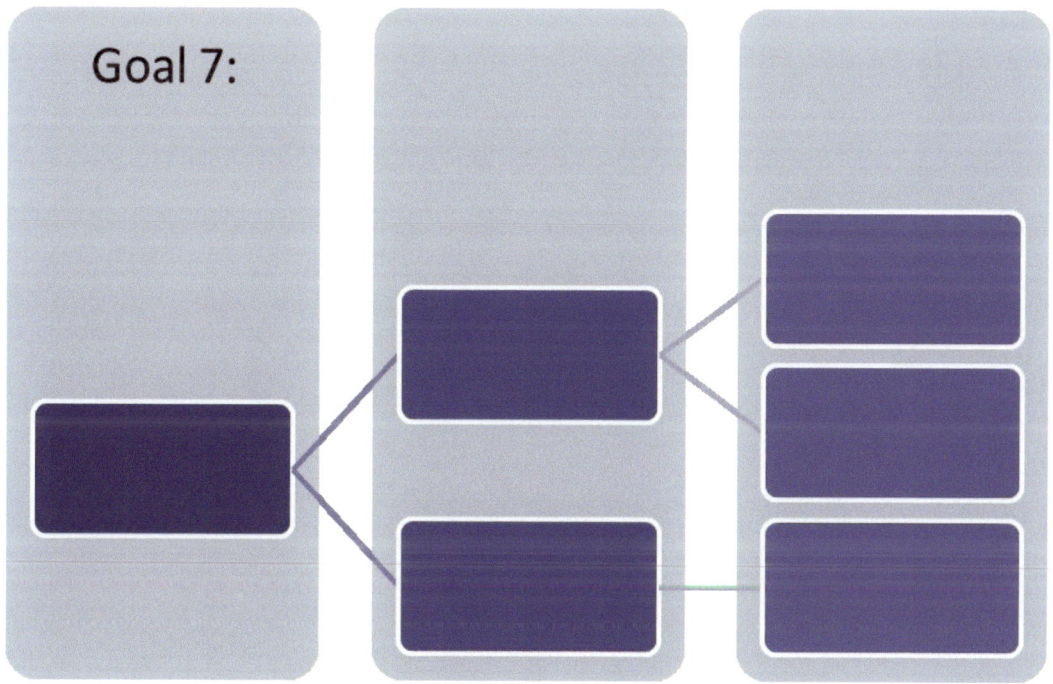

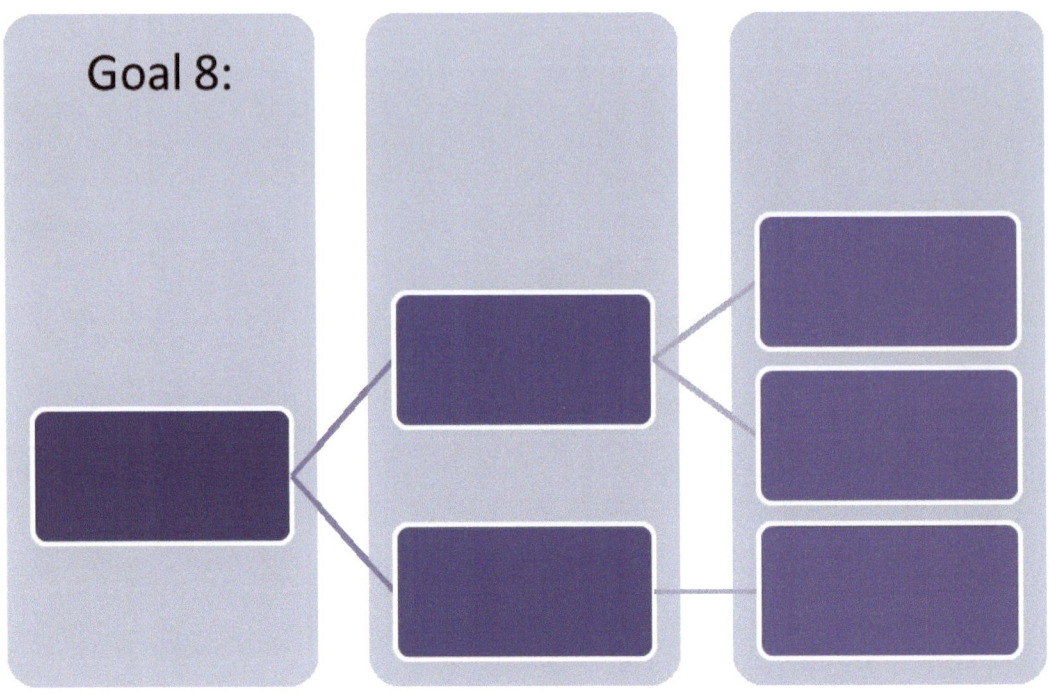
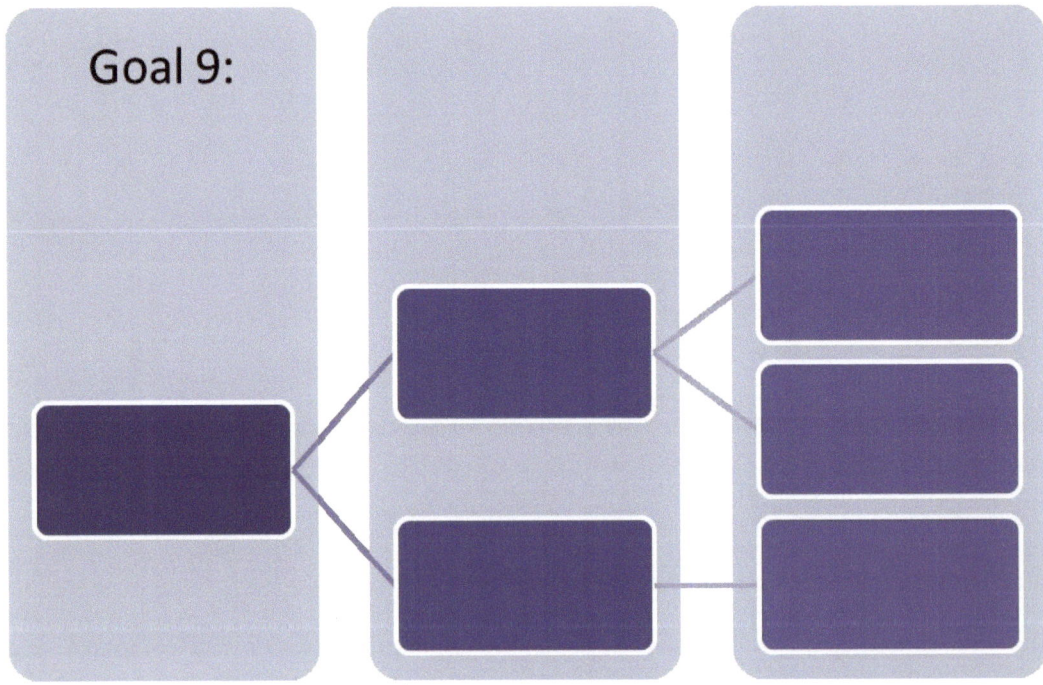

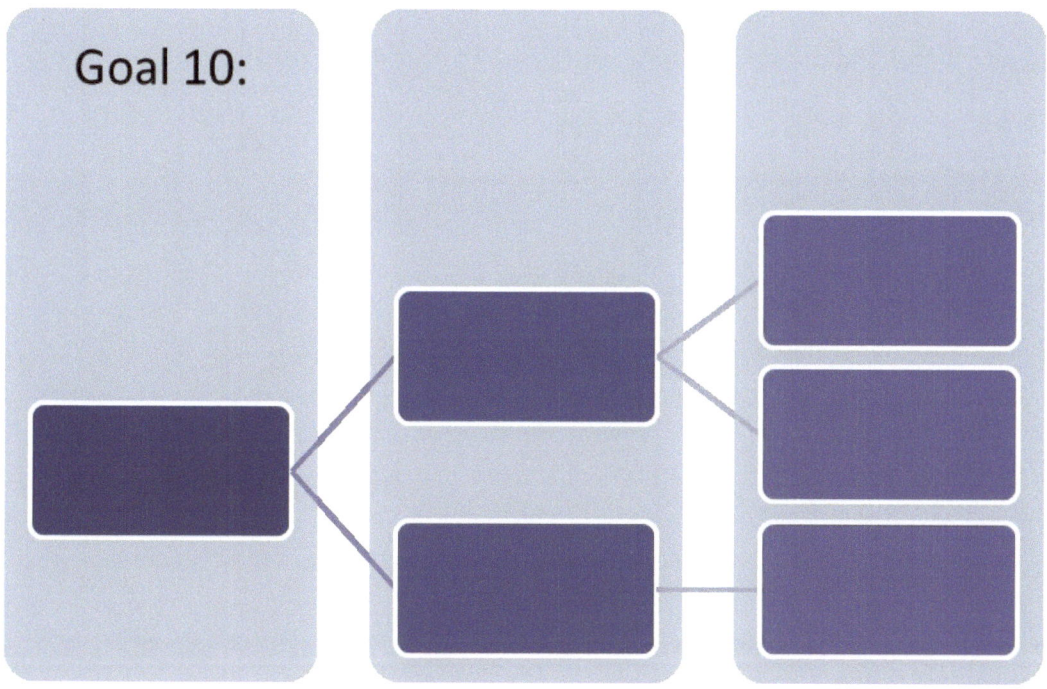

Exercise #5

The key to claiming your life back and creating order and happiness is planning. Then the next step is to place action to that plan. Step out, look into what it takes to make each goal move toward success and completion. Then begin to take those steps one by one. Soon you will turn around and need to create all new steps and plans because you will find all the old ones are complete. So as you remember that this is your life, see the vision, write it down, and listen to your heart. It can all be yours, therefore you should be living your dreams, begin to plan begin to hold the vision.

How to Do This Exercise: *Time to map out the plan.* You have resources and goals listed and now it is time to put them to work. You also have your reference point of where you are and where you want to be. Now it is time to ask these questions below. Fill them truthfully.

1. What Do I want (Goals)?_____

_____

_____

_____

_____

_____

_____

_____

_____

_____

2. When do you want it? _____

_____

_____

_____

_____

_____

_____

3. How do you want it?_____

_____

_____

_____

_____

_____

_____

_____

_____

_____

_____

_____

4. With whom do I want it? _____

_____

_____

_____

_____

_____

_____

_____

5. What are the realistic steps I can make now to get there?

    a. _____

    b. _____

    c. _____

    d. _____

6. What do I need to get there? _____

_____

_____

_____

_____

7. When will I start the plan to get there? _____

Notes

Notes

Notes

Notes

~See Yourself Whole, See Yourself Rich~

Chapter Two

Exercise #1

Something people don't understand is the fact that you have to see yourself where you want to be. You cannot say, "I want to be successful," but look in the mirror each day and see a loser. You have to see and feel the life you desire. Go to the Mercedes lot and feel the car you want, test drive it. Learn what that experience is like so that you begin to see yourself living in that experience. Dress the role you want to play; this gives you a feel for the outcome beforehand.

> **How to Do This Exercise:** *Something New.* Do something you have never done before that moves you into the feeling of one of your goals. ***Ex: If your goal is a new car, go to the car lot of the brand you most want and test drive the make and model car you desire to have. Or if you want to be a designer go to a tradeshow, dress the part and network in the industry.***

Exercise #2

What does it mean to see yourself whole? You have to see yourself with all the good the universal is pushing at you. See yourself in the beautiful houses, the new offices, in the great cars, in the wonderful marriage with the beautiful children. If you can see it you can have it, but first you must be able to see it. Something my husband and I did when we first got married was, create a vision board. We took pictures from websites that represented the things we wanted and pasted them together on a single sheet of paper and then taped it next to the bed, that way it was there before we went to bed and there when we woke up. There was no way to not see what we wanted in our lives. Praise God! Each and everything on that vision board has come into our lives over the last seven years in one way or another, and now we have an even bigger vision board with bigger dreams.

> ***How to Do This Exercise:*** *Create a vision board.* This is simple. Gather some pictures that represent or depict the things you desire to accomplish, the house, the family, maybe a picture of a gathering in a boardroom. You will place these images together on a piece of paper, cardboard, corkboard, a wall, whatever pleases you most. Then you will hang your vision board somewhere, where you can see it every day.

Exercise #3

When a client enters my company we see the potential. Our whole system works from potential, but if the client is not able or willing to see their own potential our service is useless. I have had clients tell me I expect too much, NO YOU DON'T EXPECT ENOUGH! These same clients come back to me later and are so grateful that I pushed them to see the greatness within them, their true potential. However, you may not be so lucky as to have someone like me that will coach you into your potential. That is willing to see you the way you truly are, in that case you "need" to see yourself successful because you are the only one who can.

How to Do This Exercise: *See yourself the right way.* This is really about you and the way you see you. If you don't have a positive view of yourself you will NOT receive positive results. So for the next 30 days I want you to look in the mirror each morning to give yourself positivity treatments. You will look into your own eyes and say aloud, "I am someone happy, I am great, I am successful in all I do."

Exercise #4

Feeling and seeing are the keys in this case you have to see your way to the finish line. Don't say what you can't see. That is totally irrelevant and will close the door on whatever it is you are claiming not to see. You won't see it, you know why, because you just said you can't. You have to open your eyes to your true self, to your real future. See the you that has it all, the whole you is the true you. The sooner you see yourself rich the sooner it will be. See the money in your bank accounts, see the cars in the driveway, and see the family. See your way to the top!

How to Do This Exercise: *Get in the feeling.* Go to www.LetUsBringOrder.com and download the free meditation music. As you play the music get a picture in your minds eye of what you desire to see become reality in your life. Each day you will begin to make the picture clearer in your mind until it out pictures itself into your life.

Notes

Notes

Notes

Notes

~Delete the Negatives~

Chapter Three

Exercise #1

In order to have success you have to, have to, have to delete all negativity. That means your negative thoughts as well as the negative thoughts and actions of those around you. It is hard enough trying to encourage yourself and keeping your own fears and doubts in check. You don't need the fear and doubt chorus to come help you.

People will fill your head with whatever they can to stop your progress. "Be careful, money does not grow on trees," sorry but last time I checked yes it does, where does paper come from? "Well you know you need to be good at school to finish," ok that is what studying is for to get better, pass the classes and finish, that has always been the formula for school. Every school that is honorable has tutors, if you need help it is there. "You know I tried to buy a house and that was a mess," and so was their credit, not to mention they owe tons of court fines, this has nothing to do with you. Are you seeing the point? You have to run from these conversations or don't give them a chance to breath in your life. You just don't need it!

How to Do This Exercise: *Identify the negatives.* In this exercise it is important to begin to filter out the negatives. This means people, thoughts, and habits. All the negatives that hold you back from moving in the right direction of your goals. Use the chart below to list your negatives that must be deleted.

Relataionships/People	Habits	Fears/Thoughts
• _____	• _____	• _____
• _____	• _____	• _____
• _____	• _____	• _____
• _____	• _____	• _____
• _____	• _____	• _____
• _____	• _____	• _____
• _____	• _____	• _____

Exercise #2

Strip no from your vocabulary unless using it for declining bad business ventures or unless relationships, no is not an option when it comes to your success. If you want a house so what the first 20 banks said "no", bank number 21 has that yes! You just need to look at the situation and see why the no is there, is the house you are looking at too small and you are not dreaming big enough? Are you trying to move someone that is not supposed to live with you into the house? Is it not the right neighborhood for you? It could be that the no is coming for you to make one adjustment to your plans.

You cannot play yourself short you have to get focused on your goals and see nothing but good in them. Count it all joy, even the hard times or hard roads have great lessons and opportunities. You take the nos and make them experiences for your advancement. Learn something from difficulties don't just give up. What I learned from the no with the car was that I needed a new car, not a used one. Used is not what the universe wanted for me. I deserved better.

> **How to Do This Exercise:** *Evaluate the NO.* Why are you not succeeding? Why is the no coming up? First list the area the no is coming from. Then list what the no is telling you, be candid this is the only way this will work to get a yes. Now you can look from an objective point of view to see how to produce a yes. Maybe it is time to clear some debts or your environment is wrong for your intended goal. What is your no telling you?

1. The No: Ex: <u>Car loan declined</u>   Reason for the No: Ex:

   a. <u>Have some debt that needs clearing</u>
   b. <u>This was not the car I really wanted</u>
   c. <u>I was settling for less</u>
   d. <u>Did not have enough for down payment</u>

   What is the NO telling me that will get me to my yes? Ex:

   a. <u>Clear up debt</u>
   b. <u>Go after the car I wanted</u>
   c. <u>Don't settle</u>
   d. <u>Next month is a better month to try</u>

1. The No: _____ Reason for the No:

   a. _____
   b. _____

c. _____

d. _____

What is the NO telling me that will get me to my yes?

a. _____

b. _____

c. _____

d. _____

2. The No: _____ Reason for the No:

a. _____

b. _____

c. _____

d. _____

What is the NO telling me that will get me to my yes?

a. _____

b. _____

c. _____

d. _____

3. The No: _____ Reason for the No:

a. _____

b. _____

c. _____

d. _____

What is the NO telling me that will get me to my yes?

a. _____

b. _____

c. _____

d. _____

4. The No: _____ Reason for the No:

   a. _____
   b. _____
   c. _____
   d. _____

   What is the NO telling me that will get me to my yes?

   a. _____
   b. _____
   c. _____
   d. _____

5. The No: _____ Reason for the No:

   a. _____
   b. _____
   c. _____
   d. _____

   What is the NO telling me that will get me to my yes?

   a. _____
   b. _____
   c. _____
   d. _____

6. The No: _____ Reason for the No:

   a. _____
   b. _____
   c. _____
   d. _____

What is the NO telling me that will get me to my yes?

a. _____

b. _____

c. _____

d. _____

7. The No: _____ Reason for the No:

a. _____

b. _____

c. _____

d. _____

What is the NO telling me that will get me to my yes?

a. _____

b. _____

c. _____

d. _____

8. The No: _____ Reason for the No:

a. _____

b. _____

c. _____

d. _____

What is the NO telling me that will get me to my yes?

a. _____

b. _____

c. _____

d. _____

9. The No: _____ Reason for the No:

   a. _____
   b. _____
   c. _____
   d. _____

   What is the NO telling me that will get me to my yes?

   a. _____
   b. _____
   c. _____
   d. _____

10. The No: _____ Reason for the No:

    a. _____
    b. _____
    c. _____
    d. _____

    What is the NO telling me that will get me to my yes?

    a. _____
    b. _____
    c. _____
    d. _____

Exercise #3

This is something you must get in the habit of knowing. Say it with me, "*I deserve better!*" When you start thinking to yourself, "well maybe this is too much to handle" or "I think I'm dreaming too big," stop and tell yourself, "I deserve better!" Look yourself in the mirror each morning and each evening before you go to sleep and say, "I deserve better!"

Say it so much that when negative experiences try to make their way into your life you spring into your stance and shout, "*I deserve better!*" Oh yes, this means you, "***You deserve better!***" I take these words very seriously. These words pushed me into a new season, a new experience. I decided what I was looking at was not my truth, "*I deserved better!*" Sure enough better came knocking at my door with a bow on it.

> ***How to Do This Exercise:*** *You deserve better.* Now it is a time you begin to tell yourself that you do indeed deserve better. Just before falling asleep at night begin to tell yourself over and over, "I deserve better!" You will begin to notice better appearing in your waking hours.

Exercise #4

Now some of you have business partners that display negative behavior, this will never work, but in case you get the, I am going to ride the wave partner. **86 them**! They are the main reason the business is failing. They don't believe in the vision. Some of you have partners that are there to make sure you don't succeed. Be mindful who you let in your gates. You must protect your mind gate, your ear gate and your eye gates. Don't allow people to place the fear, stress and doubt in your mind. Approach your goals with an open mind and positive thoughts. See success in every action. Know you are a great success story. Quiet the chaos by ignoring the negativity. You don't have to be rude just remove yourself from the drama, the universe will make sure they get the point and disappear.

> ***How to Do This Exercise:*** *Evaluate your relationships.* This will help with exercise 1 from this chapter. We don't always know when relationships in our lives are no good for us. This requires looking the relationship in the face to see where it needs to be placed. Some will need to be dismissed indefinitely and others you will learn to separate from your goals and dreams. Begin to ask yourself the following about the individual in your life.

Individual's name: _____

1. Do you support me? Yes/No
2. Do you talk negative about my ideas? Yes/No
3. Do you act differently when I do achieve my goals? Yes/No
4. Is your advice ever positive and insightful? Yes/No
5. Does your advice limit me? Yes/No

Individual's name: _____

1. Do you support me? Yes/No
2. Do you talk negative about my ideas? Yes/No
3. Do you act differently when I do achieve my goals? Yes/No
4. Is your advice ever positive and insightful? Yes/No
5. Does your advice limit me? Yes/No

Individual's name: _____

1. Do you support me? Yes/No
2. Do you talk negative about my ideas? Yes/No
3. Do you act differently when I do achieve my goals? Yes/No
4. Is your advice ever positive and insightful? Yes/No
5. Does your advice limit me? Yes/No

Individual's name: _____

1. Do you support me? Yes/No
2. Do you talk negative about my ideas? Yes/No
3. Do you act differently when I do achieve my goals? Yes/No
4. Is your advice ever positive and insightful? Yes/No
5. Does your advice limit me? Yes/No

Individual's name: _____

1. Do you support me? Yes/No
2. Do you talk negative about my ideas? Yes/No
3. Do you act differently when I do achieve my goals? Yes/No
4. Is your advice ever positive and insightful? Yes/No
5. Does your advice limit me? Yes/No

Individual's name: _____

1. Do you support me? Yes/No
2. Do you talk negative about my ideas? Yes/No
3. Do you act differently when I do achieve my goals? Yes/No
4. Is your advice ever positive and insightful? Yes/No
5. Does your advice limit me? Yes/No

Notes

Notes

Notes

Notes

~Handling and Circulating Your Money~

Chapter Four

Exercise #1

The biggest key to success is balance. Many fail at success because of lack of balance in business and in financing. You must create the harmony in your wallet. Come on a Journey with me so I can tell you how to create this harmony. Relax open your mind and envision yourself fully understanding the harmony in your wallet. The way to create this harmony is to stop being cheap. Truly wealthy people do not hold a tight fist. They are givers, they share their wealth. Money is not meant to be horded it is meant to circulated. That is why they call it cash flow. Something that is stored up is not being circulated it is just sitting in one place collecting unwanted dust. At the same time you are not to over circulate in any direction. The universe is created through and from order and balance. Everything has its place, time and purpose.

How to Do This Exercise: *Cash flow evaluation.* Let's see if you are circulating your money right. You should be able to evaluate this every six months. Fill in the chart below.

Your Cash Flow Now

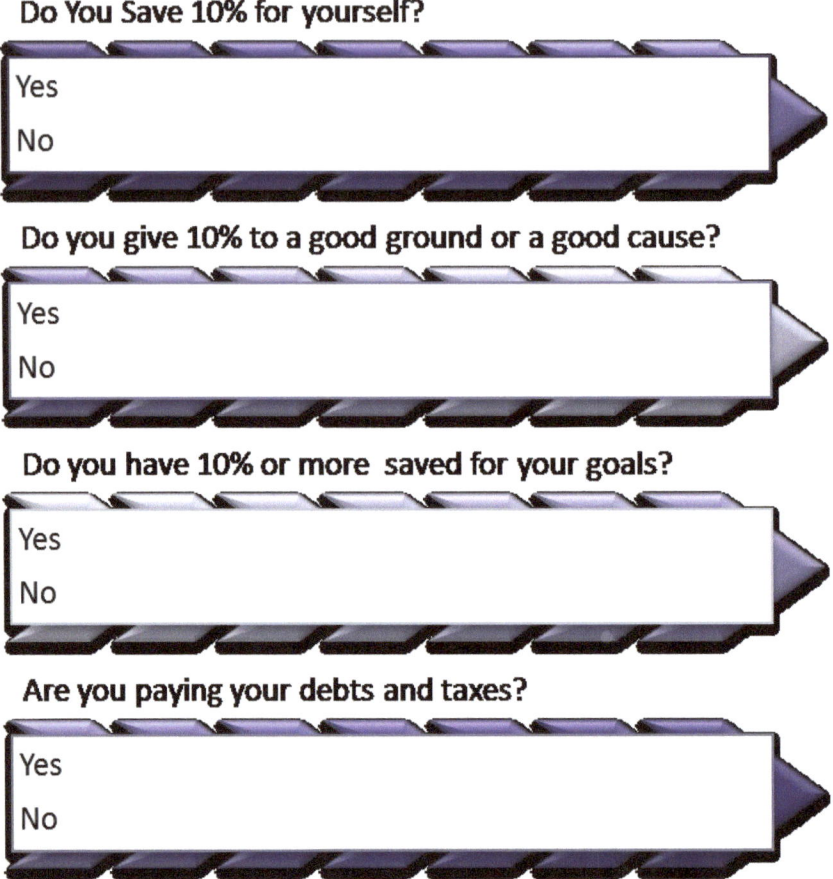

If you marked no for any of these questions then you will need to reconsider the way you have been circulating your funds. You now know the areas you need to target to create balance in the universe and your wallet.

Your Cash Flow in 6 months

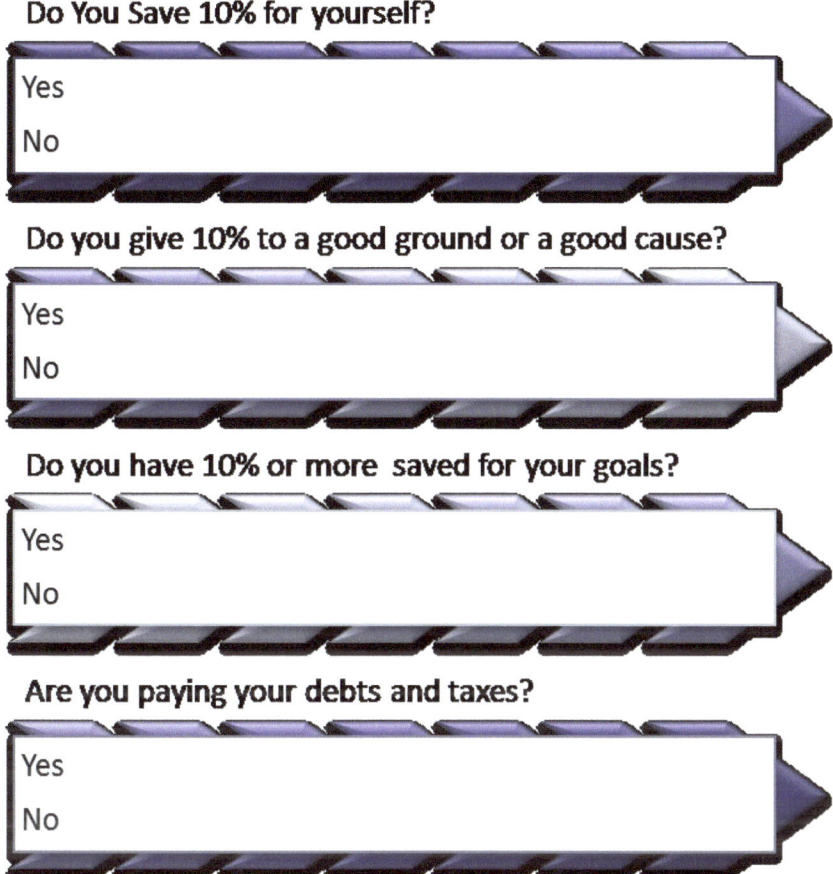

If you marked no for any of these questions this time then you really need to focus in on those areas, all must be in order. It is a must to reconsider the way you have been circulating your funds.

Your Cash Flow in 1 year

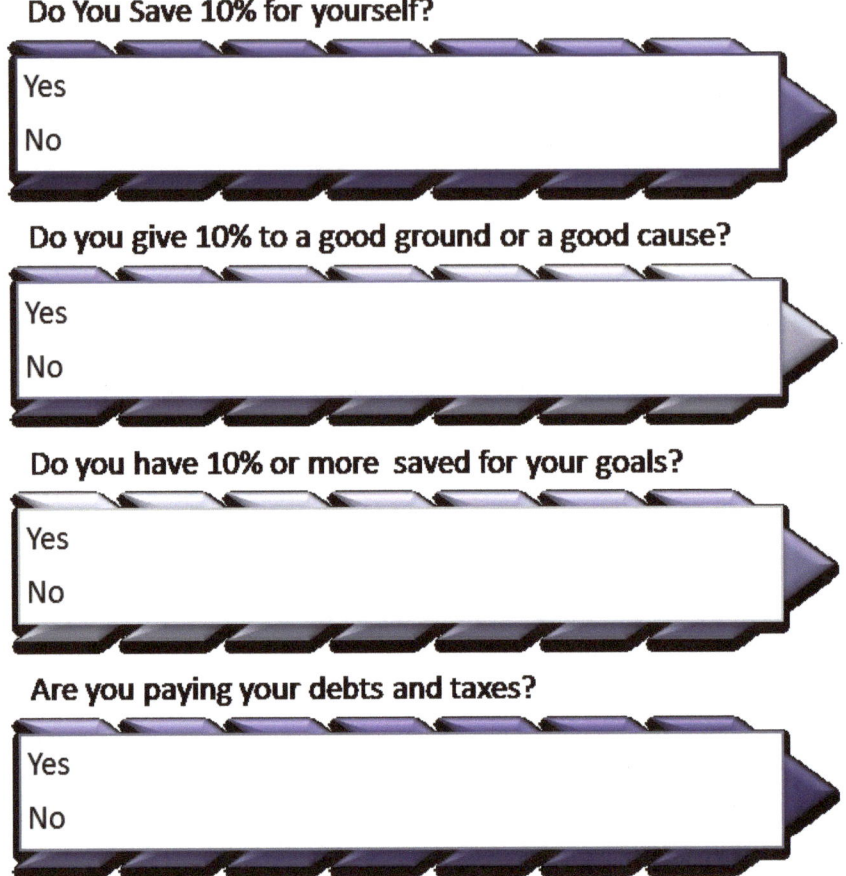

If you marked no for any of these questions by now you would really like to evaluate why you are not meeting these marks. How can you be more effective in meeting them and what is stopping you?

Exercise #2

The universe, God, does not want you to live out of balance or in that over righteous state where now you are giving him back the blessing. You are to give according to the ten percent law and then create harmony with your increase. It is really a harmony you create with your thoughts, because it is your thinking that allows you to create the size of the harvest. Your thoughts, values and predetermined limitations are what help to create the proper balance in your life.

> ***How to Do This Exercise:*** *Know the cost.* By now you should have researched your goals and you should know what it costs to move forward with the dream. This means you have a financial sheet, a list of costs for billing the idea and taking action. Use the graph below to create a financial list for each goal. You will need this to follow the instructions in exercise #3.

Item or resource needed	Cost
Ex: Printer	$199.00

Item or resource needed	*Cost*

Item or resource needed	Cost

Item or resource needed	Cost

Item or resource needed	Cost

Item or resource needed	Cost

Item or resource needed	*Cost*

Item or resource needed	Cost

Item or resource needed	Cost

Item or resource needed	Cost

Item or resource needed	Cost

Exercise #3

> ***How to Do This Exercise:*** *Take your increase to create more.* Now that you have evaluated your finances you should have created the resources to pursue your goals. You can take it a goal at a time. The cost sheets you just created in exercise #2 of this chapter gives you a look at what you need to make your goals happen. Use these sheets to take your actions with your savings. Take action on one of your goals NOW! Remember it will bring more increase when your goal is met.

Exercise #4

Answer this question; do you know why it is you do what you do? If you say it is the money you are in it for the wrong reasons. Your why is not strong enough to get you the results you seek. How many people wake up in the morning and are truly happy with what they do for a living? "Do for a living," this puts a distaste in my mouth, because most people are not working for a living, they are living to work. Most people are working on a JOB or as I love to hear it called, a "Just Over Broke," that are literally killing them. I can remember when I worked on one particular job and I would hope to get in a car accident or something just so I didn't have to go. I would wake up in the morning sick to my stomach and after a holiday or the last day of the weekend I would have the worst attitude, which by the way I did not realize until my husband made the connection at a party we attended the night before a vacation was coming to an end.

I finally realized I had lost the love I had for my job, if I ever had any. I hated it! I was there for the pay check, something I never do. I walk away from a job that makes me unhappy in a heartbeat, but here I was working for money! I quickly found a solution to that, I left and remembered to do what I loved first and make money second. I recreated the balance in my life.

How to Do This Exercise: *Are you in your passion? Do you love what you Do?* Below list what it is you want to do or what you are already doing and see if it is your passion or is it just what is paying the bills.

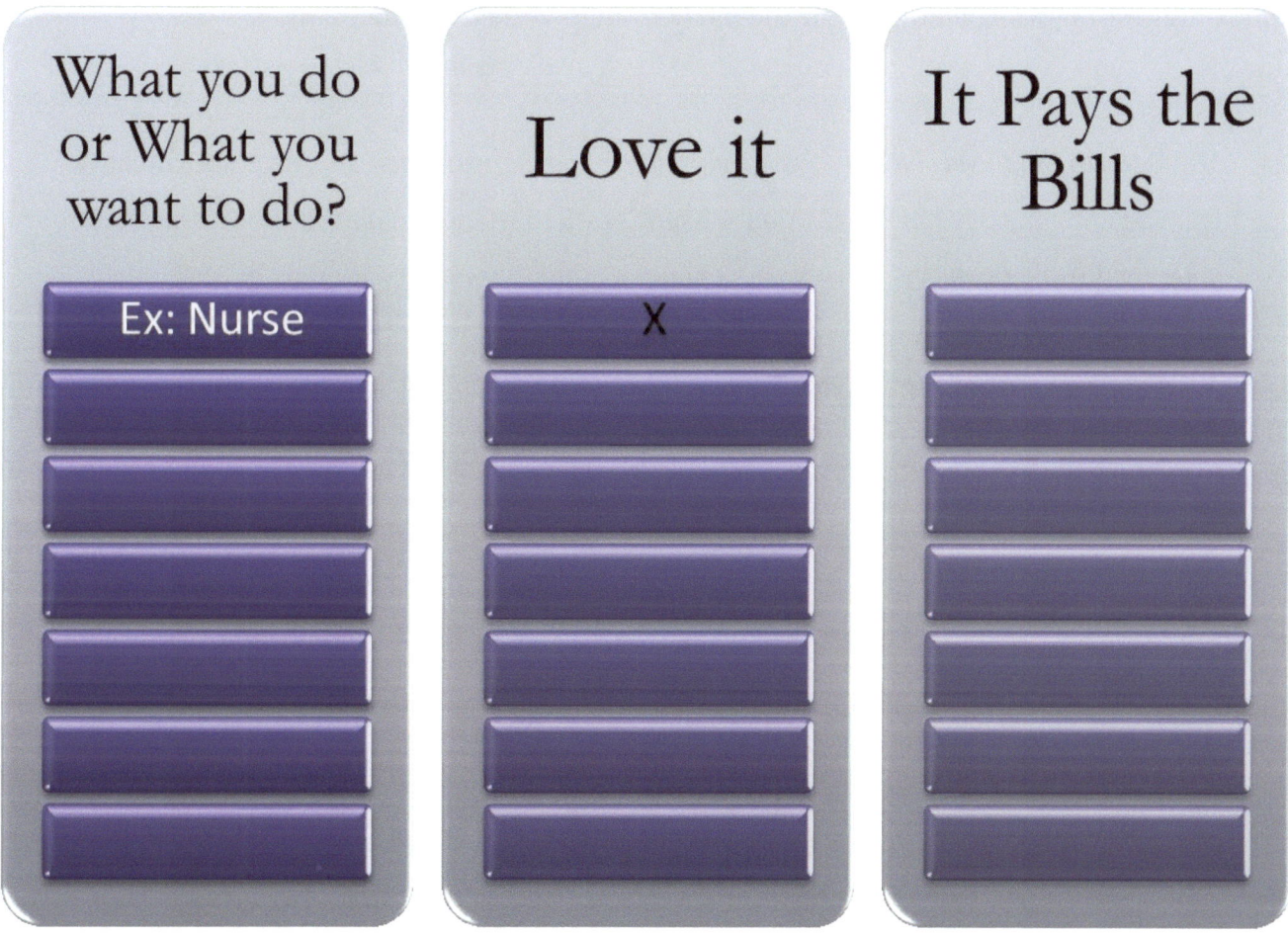

Now you know where you can make your greatest increase and what is just sustaining you for right now. You make money don't let it make you. If you love what you do it will pay you.

Exercise #5

Money also likes organization and order. This is why planning has been stressed so much. Money wants to know there is a plan for it; that you are not going to just have it sitting there doing nothing. Also keep in mind that what you plan for you receive. If you plan for a rainy day you are going to have a rainy day. You planned for it, sent out some seriously nice invitations for it. You created that very thing. So plan for things you can enjoy and money will, willingly join the party to help you enjoy the plans.

> **How to Do This Exercise:** *Always be willing to make adjustments.* At this point you have learned enough to go back to chapter 1 exercise #5 to refine the plan, add the cost sheets, and make all necessary adjustments. You may find that now your goals have changed, since you know what you love and what will pay you. Some of the other goals may not fit you any longer and that is okay. You are changing and change is good.

Exercise #6

This leads me to the four streams of income. Successful individuals have at a minimum four streams of income. Think about basketball players or any athlete. They have income from the team salary, they have endorsements, some will commentate on a sports show as well as making guest appearances. That adds up to a four, now many of the players that carry wisdom also have businesses and real estate. They understand that to maintain their luxurious lifestyle they need multiple streams of income.

How to Do This Exercise: *Four streams of Income.* Can you identify four streams of income coming into your household yet? This is four streams already coming in or four potential streams. In the chart provided below map out your streams of income.

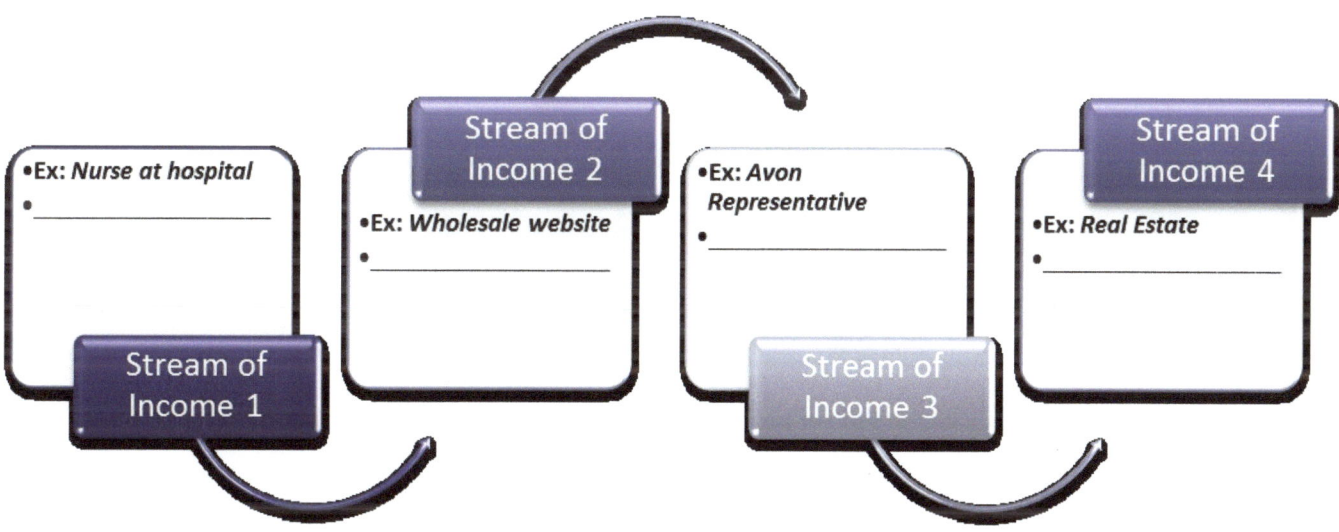

Notes

Notes

Notes

Notes

~Your Own Boss~

Chapter Five

Exercise #1

You must be willing to put the time and effort into your own career. Being afraid to ask questions or fill out the necessary paperwork is only a lie you tell yourself. Fear is the road block that needs to be destroyed in order to move forward and grow. The initial steps to becoming an entrepreneur are minimal compared to the great outcome of success and stability.

> **How to Do This Exercise:** *Setting the stage.* It is time to ask yourself the key questions that will set the stage for your goals and carrying them out. Below fill in the answers to the questions give your most straight forward answers as possible. Remember the more honest your answers are the more results you will see.

1. Where are you in the business stage?

_____
_____
_____
_____
_____

2. Do you have all the information you need? If not, why and how can you get it?

___

3. Is your paperwork in order? If not, why?

___

4. What is your next step?

___

5. Who can help you make the next step?

___

6. How soon can the next step be made?

___

7. What is after that?

___

Now take it a step at a time and do it!

Exercise #2

What a lot of people fail to think about is the future of their family. When you become your own boss you are creating an opportunity for the family. You are earning the income for the better living, the better education and the better opportunities. Your children are seeing through you what entrepreneurship truly is. In addition, your business is something they can grow into and run someday. You are modeling a successful life for your family. You are teaching your family discipline in order to grow your business.

> ***How to Do This Exercise:*** *How can I expand?* Look at your business idea or existing business, how can you expand in the next five years? Can you expand the business or do you need to create value outside the business? Write your answers to these questions below.

_____

_____

_____

_____

_____

_____

_____

Exercise #3

One thing I had to learn is that others can always see your ability for leadership. This is why they love having you around as an employee, but are not so keen on your ideas to be an entrepreneur. They want you working for them, leading their business to success. You are valuable to their company. Well guest what you are just as valuable to your own, maybe even more so because it is your baby, your creation. A true leader will teach you all they know to send you off on your way when you are ready. While building my companies I would meet people that would totally ignore my dreams and try to use my talents for their business and needs. This was a problem for me initially because I did not know how to say no or strike a balance. I should have worked to help them while I helped myself. Not! I would let them bleed me of knowledge and strength and be too tired and unfocused for my plans.

How to Do This Exercise: *Evaluate your time.* Time will only yield to you if you make it. You have to begin to organize your time even if you don't always get to move in the time frame you set for yourself. The structure here is important and will allow you to see where your time is going. Fill in the chart below to find your time.

1. Have you set time for your business?	2. Are you building on your ideas?	3. Have you defaulted on your ideas?
☐ Yes	☐ Yes	☐ Yes
☐ No	☐ No	☐ No

If you answer yes to 1 and 2 in exercise #3 you are on track and this is right where you need to be. If you said no to 1 and 2 and yes to 3 you need to make some adjustments. You are not managing your time and you a have way to go.

Exercise #4

You were born with creative money making ideas for a reason. You are meant to create, you were meant to succeed. You are meant to live a life of comfort, but it is all in your hands. Becoming your own boss opens this potential to meet your business mastery. There are so many things in life we live to master. Being able to meet mastery goals satisfies your soul and mind. So why not please yourself by taking a step. Set your mind on it, grow yourself into the idea. BE YOUR OWN BOSS.

How to Do This Exercise: *Mediate on the Boss within.* Go to www.LetUsBringOrder.com for the free mediation. Take this time to relax. Begin to see yourself as YOUR OWN BOSS.

Notes

Notes

Notes

Notes

~Why Four Streams~

Chapter Six

Earlier on you heard me speak of four streams of income. I would like to touch on the concept a little more here. I learned this from my mentor and then put it on steroids. If you ever read the bible in the book of Genesis it speaks of the main river that broke into four streams that flowed out of the Garden of Eden. *[10]And a river went out of Eden to water the garden; and from thence it was parted, and became into four heads. [11]The name of the first is Pison: that is it which compasseth the whole land of Havilah, where there is gold; [12]And the gold of that land is good: there is bdellium and the onyx stone. [13]And the name of the second river is Gihon: the same is it that compasseth the whole land of Ethiopia. [14]And the name of the third river is Hiddekel: that is it which goeth toward the east of Assyria. And the fourth river is Euphrates* (Genesis 2: 10-14). These four streams kept the flow, watered and nourished. Don't you want to live a life that is watered and nourished?

Your finances should support and work with each other. If you have a well-balanced cash flow you have no concern for lack. Balance! Balance usually comes in fours. North, South, East and West. Summer, Winter, Spring and Fall. A table or chairs for that matter has four legs.

The number four is a number of increase. Think about it 2 plus 2 equals four. 2 time 2 equals four. You always want to add or multiple in your life. The number four represents foundation. Having four streams of income creates a strong foundation. Your foundation is what keeps you standing.

> ***How to Do This Exercise:*** *Create your own Matrix.* The goal here is to find your cash flow by mapping out your income flow. The example chart below shows the flow of income. Fill in the next chart according to the stream description below.

To explain the matrix it is important to understand the four sections, the Potential Streams are where you are listing your income that has potential to grow and behave as resources in your finances. However, this stream still need your support and attention to grow and provide you with the expansion you are looking for. This income could be a website you have started that is making great money but is not able to make money while you are sleeping just yet. You still have to give more attention than you are comfortable with for this stream. However, your potential income can grow into jackpot income.

Questionable streams are not as yielding, there is growth in this income but it is also a risk income. There are high demands with this income but little return in the broader spectrum. This would refer to incomes like investments, investment properties, etc. If you cannot stabilize these incomes quickly then they become slackers. You will end up paying a heavy investment into a questionable stream or you will have to sell or get rid of it.

Jackpot streams will not necessarily grow but it is your more mature and stable income. This stream should be generating a lot of cash flow into your home. This would most likely be your main source of income and it helps to fund your other streams. This is the position you are striving to get your passion in.

Slacker streams are streams of income that really are not growing. You want to avoid these incomes as much as possible. These are the get rich fast ideas that cost more to workout then you can afford or are willing to invest, whether it is time or money.

Take your time to fill in the chart now see where your income is.

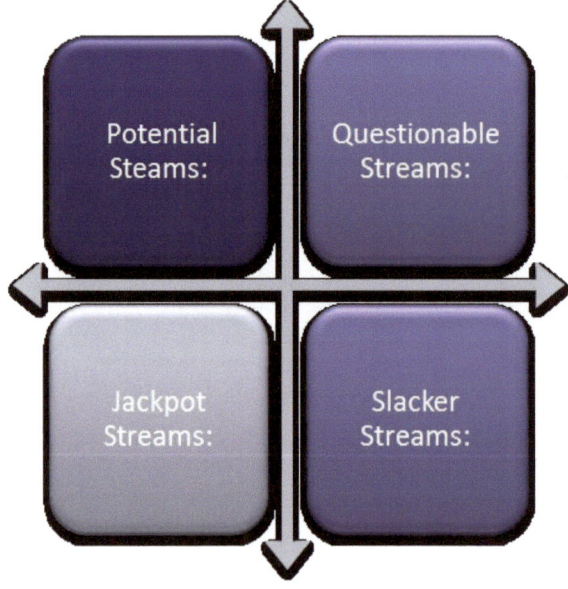

Exercise #2

In *Let Us Bring Order* the book spoke of Joe and his streams of income. We understand that at any time one of the four streams Joe is now maintaining can lack steady income flow, but with the generation of the other three it gives Joe room to breathe and to think about what is going on around him. If the Internet services fall in profits in April Joe does not need to sweat. He has just become aware that changes need to happen. Increase in marketing the Internet service, a web party, perhaps new computers or maybe it is time to remove the Internet and bring in live entertainment.

> **How to Do This Exercise:** *What is my income telling me?* Your income is always speaking. You must learn how to listen to your income and the secrets it is sharing with you. Answer the questions below and see what your income is telling you right now.

1. Do you have four streams of income? If not how many do you have?

   _____
   _____
   _____
   _____
   _____

2. What are your options for more streams?

   a. _____
   b. _____
   c. _____
   d. _____
   e. _____
   f. _____
   g. _____

3. How can you get some more streams up and running?

   _____
   _____
   _____
   _____
   _____

4. Is a stream currently warning you it is time to evaluate your income? Ex: Cuts in hours, or demand for your services. Sometimes warnings come just to make you aware of your need to add more streams and once you handle the threat the first streams corrects itself.

_____
_____
_____
_____

5. What can you do now to watch your streams?

_____
_____
_____
_____
_____
_____

Exercise #3

It is much easier than you think to produce four streams of income. Having a rental property or two is a good start. If you invest wisely, picking up a piece of property in a great area, which you managed to get for a great price, you are in the money. Your maintenance fees are so minimal you are walking away with a monthly steal. And this is possible because you planned ahead. You studied the real estate to see that this would truly be another stream of income for you.

This system also creates checks and balances in your finances. When you see a stream that is drying you begin to question the waters before it is too late. Can your other streams save the one or will the one diminish the others? Never become complacent with your cash flow. When you do, you become the boiling frog. You are sitting in the pot not noticing that the water is getting hotter and hotter until it is too late and you are cooked.

Let your four streams become your eyes and ears, your indicators. Keep an eye on the changes to your wealth so that you know how to change. Let the cushion of the four streams helps you remain in the driver's seat but notice when the cushion is telling you it needs to be reupholstered.

> ***How to Do This Exercise:*** *Your Streams.* It is easier to work your streams of income if you can see them. How can you break down your passion into four streams? This concept can even begin to add to your other incomes. We are now taking one of four and expanding it. You can teach others your skills or develop a product, if you blog about cars, brand your own wax or tools. There is always room for growth and if there isn't, you need to rethink the stream; it will be the first to give you issues. Let's see if you can take your four streams and figure out how you can generate four streams from the original four. In the chart provided begin to map out your streams of income so you can see where you are where you need to be.

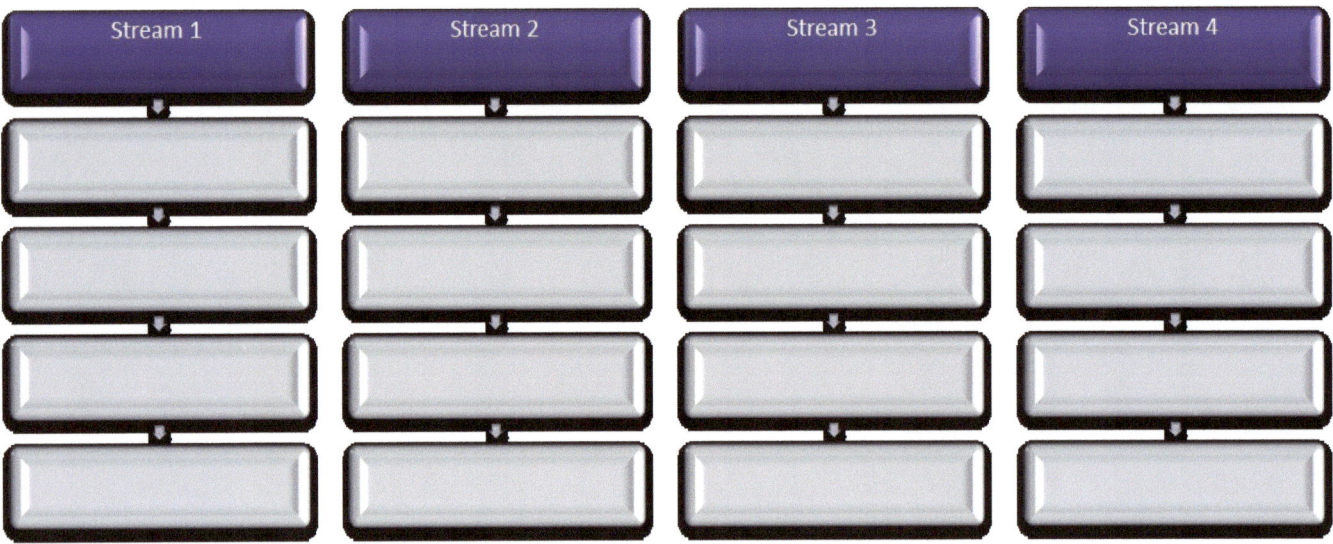

Exercise #3

Why four streams? So your well doesn't run dry. Four streams of income is just another form of planning your goals and your way to success. Take time to evaluate your streams of income. If you are ready to finally build wealth and success be honest with yourself about these questions. Don't get caught without a stream.

> **How to Do This Exercise:** *Review your streams.* The questions below are to help you put what you have learned into perspective. If you are ready to finally build wealth and success be honest with yourself about these questions.

1. How many streams are flowing into your home?

_____
_____
_____

2. Is there at least one stream from everyone in the home? List them.

_____
_____
_____
_____
_____

3. How can you increase those streams?

___

4. How many of those streams are coming from your passion?

___

Notes

Notes

Notes

Notes

~Money "Matters"~

Chapter Seven

Exercise #1

I thought it would be a great idea to show you the truth and purpose of money. So first let's throw away all the garbage about money being evil. The last time I went to the store to get food I needed money. To top that, I don't remember the twenty dollar bill bursting into flames or giving me a sinister laugh when it came out of my pocketbook. Money is what we use to get things. Money is a friend, but are you being a friend to money?

Stop saying what you don't need! If you did not need money you would not be reading this book. No one is impressed by poverty so stop trying to be modest about your desires. Yes, you would like to have a nice new expensive car. Yes, you do want a nice new house. Yes, you do want a vacation. Yes, you would like to pay all your bills on time and still have money for food and a shopping spree at the mall. But if you continue to lie to yourself and the universe that all you need is this or all you need is that, guess what this and that is all you are going to get.

> ***How to Do This Exercise:** Deal with your vocabulary.* It is time to renegotiate with the universe. You must take back all the bad programming you sent out on your behalf. You are programming your life everyday with your thoughts and words. So now is the time to reprogram your life.
>
> Begin to think about all the negative things you have thought or said. I don't need….. I don't have……. I can live without ……. This is the programming that is holding you back.
>
> Get a blank piece of paper. I want you to begin to write down your negative programming. Make sure you get it all down. Now is the fun part. I want you to destroy this paper. Tear it up, ball it up, burn it in the fireplace (be mindful when using fire), whatever really moves you to know these programs are destroyed from your experience for good. Then say out loud, "Cancel, cancel, cancel," to those negative thoughts and words and know that they cannot come back."

Exercise #2

It is time to stop focusing on where the money is coming from for a minute and just focus on the fact that it is here. Money is your friend, it has missed you dearly and wants to treat you to some new things, take you to some new places. Introduce you to her other friends and family. Think about it money can do all of this for you. All money wants you to do is realize that money matters. Money is not filthy, it is not evil; it is a friend indeed. I don't know about you but I could use a few friends that want to take me out shopping.

Money only requires that you respect it. Not worship, respect. We give respect where respect is do. How do you know the difference? When you can walk away from something you have mastered it. You are at a point where you are not worshipping a thing. It is not the master of you. When you can walk away from a million dollar deal because you know it is wrong and the deal will harm more than it will help you are mastering money. You are placing money where you should, because anything, anyone that loves you can leave your life but it will always return. That million dollars will know you had respect for it and others around you, it will seek you out and make its way into your life in a good and appreciate manner because you did not bad mouth the money you turned down the deal. You placed the value in the right order.

> ***How to Do This Exercise:*** *Money is in the mind.* **Money needs to become a part of your thought process. We should mediate upon those things we desire to see. Take some time for yourself to mediate on the wealthy you. Download money mediation from www.LetUsBringOrder.com**

Exercise #3

Stop bad mouthing money. I mean this. It is insane to look at money as the cause of a problem. This takes us back to accountability. The two million dollar car did not run the light and cause the accident, the driver did. The twelve million dollar salary did not make the CEO harass the secretary. He decided to do that on his own. Nine times out of ten if he was a manager at Wendy's he would have sexually harassed a worker there as well. If you are looking at a situation that seems like money caused it, look a little deeper. I bet your fingerprints are all over the problem. You created that mess somehow, and now my friend money is taking the blame. Well I have news for you, money does not like being blamed for things it did not do and as long as you blame her, she is not going to come around.

> ***How to Do This Exercise:*** *The true root of your evil.* This is a real grown up exercise. You are accountable for you. Let's really find the root of your problem. What is holding you back?

1. If money was not an issue, *(which it is not)*, what would be the next step that you have not taken?

   _____
   _____
   _____
   _____
   _____

2. Is there a step before that, that you have ignored or broken the law to?

   _____
   _____
   _____
   _____
   _____

3. If all prerequisites are in place what choice can you make that will move you forward?

_____
_____
_____
_____

4. Have you stopped blaming everything else and find the solution yet?

_____
_____
_____

Excuses are guarded lies, what lie is blocking you!!!

Notes

Notes

Notes

Notes

~Taste the Success~

Chapter Eight

Exercise #1

Now that we have placed the mind in order and have the focus necessary to plan and attract the money for the plan, it is time to hit the ground running. We are at the point where the plan is finished and you are ready to put yourself out there.

Whatever the goal maybe, the key to getting to the finish line is to start. I studied project management during my MBA studies. I have a Master's in Business, in marketing and project management. One of the tasks in strategic planning and project management is to plan implementation. See it is understood that people plan and plan and plan and guess what they never move beyond that plan. Well this is not going to be you. You have put your heart into this plan and you owe it to yourself to step out on your plan.

> ***How to Do This Exercise:*** *Implementation.* Now it is time to implement the plan you have created. Ask yourself the questions below to see where are your next steps?

1. What are the desired outcomes?

   _____
   _____
   _____
   _____

2. When will you start them?

   _____
   _____
   _____
   _____

3. When do you plan to finish?

   _____
   _____
   _____
   _____
   _____
   _____
   _____

4. What do you need to start?

_____
_____
_____
_____
_____

Exercise #2

You have to make a move. If you set the goal to go college, you have apply to the schools, you have to research which schools are best for you and your major. Though I would love to help I can't do it for you nor can anyone else. You have to say this is it, "I am taking control."

Maybe your goal is to start an Internet business. By now you should have the vision on paper and now is the time to tighten that vision up by moving on the site, put together your marketing tools and begin telling people about your site. It is on you to start things up.

> ***How to Do This Exercise:*** *List Your Outcomes, make them plane.* In exercise #2 you will be able to take this format and create a graph to map out the methods you will use to complete your implementation. Fill in the spaces provided.

● **Outcome ~ _Ex: Start New Business_**

    Step ~ _Ex: Paperwork_

        Tasks ~

            a) _Ex: Research_
            b) _Ex: File paperwok_
            c)
            d)

● **Outcome ~** _____

    Step 1 ~ _____

        Tasks ~

            a) _____
            b) _____
            c) _____
            d) _____

    Step 2 ~ _____

        Tasks ~

            a) _____
            b) _____
            c) _____
            d) _____

    Step 3 ~ _____

Tasks ~

    a) _____
    b) _____
    c) _____
    d) _____

*Step 4 ~*_____

  Tasks ~

    a) _____
    b) _____
    c) _____
    d) _____

*Outcome ~*_____

*Step 1 ~*_____

  Tasks ~

    a) _____
    b) _____
    c) _____
    d) _____

*Step 2 ~*_____

  Tasks ~

    a) _____
    b) _____
    c) _____

d) _____

*Step 3 ~*_____

   Tasks ~

      a) _____
      b) _____
      c) _____
      d) _____

*Step 4 ~*_____

   Tasks ~

      a) _____
      b) _____
      c) _____
      d) _____

*Outcome ~*_____

   *Step 1 ~*_____

     Tasks ~

        a) _____
        b) _____
        c) _____
        d) _____

   *Step 2 ~*_____

Tasks ~

    a) _____

    b) _____

    c) _____

    d) _____

*Step 3 ~*_____

  Tasks ~

    a) _____

    b) _____

    c) _____

    d) _____

*Step 4 ~*_____

  Tasks ~

    a) _____

    b) _____

    c) _____

    d) _____

*Outcome ~*_____

*Step1 ~*_____

  Tasks ~

    a) _____

    b) _____

    c) _____

d) _____

Step 2 ~ _____

   Tasks ~

      a) _____
      b) _____
      c) _____
      d) _____

Step 3 ~ _____

   Tasks ~

      a) _____
      b) _____
      c) _____
      d) _____

Step 4 ~ _____

   Tasks ~

      a) _____
      b) _____
      c) _____
      d) _____

Outcome ~ _____

   Step1 ~ _____

      Tasks ~

         a) _____
         b) _____
         c) _____
         d) _____

   Step 2 ~ _____

      Tasks ~

         a) _____
         b) _____
         c) _____
         d) _____

   Step 3 ~ _____

      Tasks ~

         a) _____
         b) _____
         c) _____
         d) _____

   Step 4 ~ _____

      Tasks ~

         a) _____
         b) _____
         c) _____

d) _____

Outcome ~ _____

Step1 ~ _____

Tasks ~

    a) _____
    b) _____
    c) _____
    d) _____

Step 2 ~ _____

Tasks ~

    a) _____
    b) _____
    c) _____
    d) _____

Step 3 ~ _____

Tasks ~

    a) _____
    b) _____
    c) _____
    d) _____

*Step 4 ~*_____

    Tasks ~

        a) _____
        b) _____
        c) _____
        d) _____

*Outcome ~*_____

    *Step1 ~*_____

        Tasks ~

            a) _____
            b) _____
            c) _____
            d) _____

    *Step 2 ~*_____

        Tasks ~

            a) _____
            b) _____
            c) _____
            d) _____

    *Step 3 ~*_____

        Tasks ~

            a) _____
            b) _____

c) _____

d) _____

*Step 4 ~*_____

Tasks ~

a) _____

b) _____

c) _____

d) _____

*Outcome ~*_____

*Step1 ~*_____

Tasks ~

a) _____

b) _____

c) _____

d) _____

*Step 2 ~*_____

Tasks ~

a) _____

b) _____

c) _____

d) _____

*Step 3 ~*_____

    Tasks ~

        a) _____
        b) _____
        c) _____
        d) _____

*Step 4 ~*_____

    Tasks ~

        a) _____
        b) _____
        c) _____
        d) _____

*Outcome ~*_____

*Step1 ~*_____

    Tasks ~

        a) _____
        b) _____
        c) _____
        d) _____

*Step 2 ~*_____

    Tasks ~

        a) _____
        b) _____

c) _____

d) _____

*Step 3 ~*_____

Tasks ~

a) _____

b) _____

c) _____

d) _____

*Step 4 ~*_____

Tasks ~

a) _____

b) _____

c) _____

d) _____

*Outcome ~*_____

*Step 1 ~*_____

Tasks ~

a) _____

b) _____

c) _____

d) _____

*Step 2 ~*_____

   Tasks ~

      a) _____
      b) _____
      c) _____
      d) _____

*Step 3 ~*_____

   Tasks ~

      a) _____
      b) _____
      c) _____
      d) _____

*Step 4 ~*_____

   Tasks ~

      a) _____
      b) _____
      c) _____
      d) _____

Exercise #3

With every step you take, you are getting to taste a piece of your success. You are getting to a place of accomplishment. This is when determination kicks in because you are seeing the dream take shape. Every tiny piece of the picture creates the whole. You will find your frame full in no time; if you stick to the principles you have been given you will soar.

> ***How to Do This Exercise:*** *Success is sweet and the sweetness is reached by following the formula.* Begin to use this formula in your life and you will see the results come to life.

Formula to Success:

1. Sow the seed.
   - Start with your ten percent.
   - Now Stretch.
   - Empty out into good ground.
2. Plan.
   - Set your goals.
   - Write a plan.
   - Research.
3. See yourself where you want to be.
   - Let no one stop you.
   - Trim the fat, get rid of distractions.
4. Become friends with money.
   - See money in the right way.
5. Make a step.

Exercise #4

Once again don't limit yourself. You can have all you can handle in this life. Just see and believe. Once you have decided what success is to you see yourself in it. I was once told by someone who loves me very much to dream big as big as I could and I started to see things I was not aware of before I was able to pull the limits off and see great things for myself. You have to see your supply, taste it and it will meet your demand.

> **How to Do This Exercise:** *Finding your center of strengthen.* Download the mediation for this exercise from www.LetUsBringOrder.com

Once you get your first taste you will know it is too good to go back. Let success be your motivator. Let your first taste take you to the next level.

Notes

Notes

Notes

Notes

~Mediation – Relaxation~

Chapter Nine

Exercise #1

I would be doing you a great disservice if I fail to touch on mediation and relaxation. You need the two to bring harmony to self. You must find the time to reset yourself daily. One reason some people are happy today and a mess tomorrow is because they fail to reset their thoughts and their focus.

> **How to Do This Exercise:** *Clear your mind.* Listen to mediation to clear your thoughts. You need to set our emotions aside in order to get in alignment with your path to success. You can download the mediation from www.LetUsBringOrder.com

Exercise #2

So what are you worrying about? Is it the bills, not finding a mate, or maybe failing a class? What you mediate on will become your reality. Now do you see why mediation is important? You must become aware of mediation in order to prevent mediating on the wrong things. Don't say you don't have time to mediate because you are doing it already all day long.

> **How to Do This Exercise:** *What thoughts are creeping in the shadows?* Make a list of the things you feel are not going as they should. Now let's evaluate the thoughts you have around that area.

What is going wrong: **Ex:** <u>Car trouble</u>

Thoughts: **Ex:** <u>I need a new car I've had this car to long. All my neighbors have such nice cars. I'm embarrassed of my car.</u>

Are you seeing how your thoughts can affect your life.

- *What is going wrong:* _____
_____
_____

    Thoughts: _____
    _____
    _____

- *What is going wrong:* _____
_____
_____

    Thoughts: _____
    _____
    _____

● **What is going wrong:** _____
_____
_____

    Thoughts: _____
    _____
    _____
    _____

● **What is going wrong:** _____
_____
_____

    Thoughts: _____
    _____
    _____

● **What is going wrong:** _____
_____
_____

    Thoughts: _____
    _____
    _____
    _____

● *What is going wrong:* _____
_____
_____

Thoughts: _____
_____
_____
_____

● *What is going wrong:* _____
_____
_____

Thoughts: _____
_____
_____

Exercise #3

If you are looking for the next step in your business, sit quietly and ask in your mind "what is my next step?" The answer will come to you with time. Sometimes it will be a quick response other times you will have to put in sometime. I found it good to write your questions down before you go into mediation, but that's me. I do this because sometimes I go in for one thing and I come out with so much more. I get answers to things and get excited and forget all about my original entry assignment.

> ***How to Do This Exercise:*** *Take time to ask yourself some questions in mediation.* Get a notebook and pen, find a place where you can relax. Still your mind and focus on the peace within. Now ask yourself the following:

1. What is it you want to move with first?

   _____
   _____
   _____
   _____

2. What is the next step?

   _____
   _____
   _____
   _____

3. How can you plan more to insure success?

   _____
   _____
   _____
   _____
   _____
   _____

4. Who can help you on this journey? Who do you need to release?

   _____
   _____
   _____
   _____
   _____
   _____

Notes

Notes

Notes

Notes

~Mentors and Mentorship~

Chapter Ten

Exercise#1

I know I have mentioned my mentor a few times. He always says you should not move through life without a guide. I firmly believe in this truth. When you were in middle school you had a teacher. Your teacher went to school to learn to teach and became certified to teach you. They had to have experience to teach you. The school was not going to let the girl sitting next to you get up and take over the class for the year. This is the concept you should keep throughout life, you need someone that has been where you are trying to go.

Personally, when I set a goal I want to find the person who has accomplished that goal on a mastery level and get them to guide me through the process into success. I don't want the advice of someone that is moving in the same lane as me. I need someone with experience, someone that has seen the finish line and knows how I can get to the finish line as well. This individual will not only know how to get through but they will know to tell me which direction will be trouble and which steps I can avoid to stay out of trouble. It won't be a case of the blind leading the blind if you find a mentor that will lead you from experience.

How to Do This Exercise: Research time. Look at your goals. Answer the questions below to get a clear view.

1. Can you find at least two individuals that can help guide you to the finish line successfully?

_____
_____
_____
_____
_____
_____

2. Do you have their books?

_____
_____
_____
_____
_____
_____
_____

3. Are you following their methods?

_____
_____
_____
_____
_____

4. Can you gain access to have them mentor you?

_____
_____
_____
_____
_____

5. Have you research the best, the moguls, the titans in your industry?

_____
_____
_____
_____
_____

Exercise #2

There is nothing wrong with a guide, nothing wrong with saying, "I don't know it all, but I want to learn." Most people want to walk it alone thinking they know it all or know better than everyone else. Even kings have advisors. Having a guide gets you to your goals faster. You are not going to hold yourself accountable the way a great mentor will. My clients know that some days I am the last person they want to see or talk to but when I am done they are going to love me and the hell I put them through because I see the place they want to go and I know how to get them there. It's my job to push them the extra mile to make sure they meet their goals.

You should also make it a point to seek not only all the writings of your mentor, which will show you their evolution, but find out what they are reading and have read. This will give you insight to so much and will help you understand where your mentor is coming from and where they are going, as well as where they are leading you.

Everyone Needs A Guide!

How to Do This Exercise: *More Research.* Treat yourself to wisdom. Find at least two books a month that can provide insight to your goals. Begin to highlight and markup all the details that will help you with your success.

Notes

Notes

Notes

Notes

~Becoming A Mentor~

Chapter Eleven

Exercise #1

Now that you have a mentor you are on your way to becoming a master. First off, no you are not going to master anything in a week, month or year, it takes about 10 years to master anything, studies say that it take 10,000 hours to master a skill. I guess now you understand why you don't disconnect from your mentor to early.

When becoming a master taking shortcuts that you have made up is a dangerous move. It only tacks on more time to your journey most times your shortcuts develops a bad habit that has to be unlearned before you move forward again. I like to ask my clients their goals and find out what they are moving to master. Then I like to find out the steps they have taken to get there. This allows me to see how much time they have already put into their goal and to see what steps were taken and which were skipped. Then I am able to work from there. I know their strengthens and weaknesses and I can help them connect or reconnect with their goals.

> **How to Do This Exercise:** *Ready to Master your dreams?* Take a look at what it is you really want to master. As you do so you are going to see what it is you have to address to make sure you are a master and not copycat or a fluke.

1. What are you looking to master?

2. What steps have you taken?

3. What have you skipped? Be honest with yourself.

_____
_____
_____
_____
_____
_____
_____
_____

Exercise #2

If you desire to be a music artist I want to know how many songs you have written, how many you have recorded if any, how long have you been singing, have you had training, are you being trained now? Are you seeing the point, in order to master singing you have to have been moving toward it somehow in some way? You don't just wake up one day and decide oh I am going to be a great singer. Sure you may have a real natural talent but that is only part of the puzzle. You need to learn to master that talent. Learn to sing in the recording studio, in stadiums, in small settings.

You can master anything you set your mind to. You just have to find the drive and determination. Once determination kicks in you are on your way. Nothing will stop you. I have become that way about life. I am determined to be a master of my own destiny and a master of change. That is why I am sort after as a consultant. I have mastered change and the ability to create order. What are you mastering? What are you putting the time and effort into?

Whatever it is you desire to accomplish the ability for you to master it is there. Maybe you didn't realize before this that you wanted to master something or that you even could, but now you know and it is your time to go out there and put the time in. Make the time for your passion. Find the mentor that is going to push you to your mastery zone and soar to new levels that used to only exist in your imagination. Become the prima, the black belt, the master in your arena.

> ***How to Do This Exercise:*** *Time to put in time.* Begin devoting time to your passion. You now know what you have done to achieve mastery and what you have neglected so now let's move toward doing this right and getting to what you need to complete. Begin with a day a week if necessary, this is where you devote sometime to your passion. You can then begin to increase time from there, once you have disciplined yourself.

Notes

Notes

Notes

Notes

~New Beginnings~

Chapter Twelve

I want to thank you for believing in yourself and taking this journey with me. I know you are well on your way to being the success I know you are and that you see yourself being. Wash your hands of the past, because that is what it is, the past. You can't do anything with it so leave it where it is. Don't look back. Forgive yourself and the others that were players or characters in those seasons. You are starting fresh.

This is your new beginning. Don't let anything stop you. You are now a serious sower. You have your goals and you're your own boss. You know how to treat money. You are sitting under the right mentor and you are working toward mastery. You have even taken advantage of going to www.LetUsBringOrder.com to start up your membership and I see you getting really serious and seeking more help at www.rennyconsulting.com. I know that sounds like a new you to me.

Relax and don't worry about the people you can't take along. The right friendships and relationships will show up all around you. You just need to be ready. I am excited for you. You are building a strong foundation and your hard work will pay off, and when I meet you at the top I will know we took this journey together and you were one of the willing students.

Remember, this will mean as much to you as you open up and allow yourself to receive. If you have read this looking to receive nothing then that is what you will walk away with. But if you read this book open to change and to have a chance to bring order, you will walk away with wealth beyond wealth. This book has shown you the keys to the palace and you will take them right to the doorway.

You will be the same one that seeks further knowledge and wealth. You will need to see more secrets, gain more revelation and I will be awaiting your return. For the teacher appears when the student is ready.

Your new beginning comes with a season of willingness to expand and learn. Your eyes have opened to the potential of more. To the possibility of a new life, order awaits you. You and your family will thank you for taking this journey. Understand that there is no turning back for you. You have opened a door that is inviting you in and once you walk in you will want to stay and find your way to the next door and you shall. You shall find the next door and begin to plan your way to the one after that. The joy you receive from meeting your goals will compel you to make a new set and start the journey once again.

This is your life and it is time you begin to live as if this is not about anything or anyone else. Others will benefit from your success but you will first have to focus on you to get you to the success.

Once again I thank you for loving yourself enough to start this change. May your life be filled with wealth, health and prosperity. See yourself as you want others to see you and dream big.

Make your next step by going to www.rennyconsulting.com

Notes

Notes

Notes

Notes

Notes

ABOUT THE AUTHOR

Verleiz Lattimore was born in New York, growing up with a well-rounded education and understanding of people. After several years of working for the Board of Education Verleiz found herself ready to breakout of the box, following the devastation of losing her mother to cancer, which started an extreme chain of events leading to a spiritual transformation and growth. Mrs. Lattimore now is very active in ministry and counseling, while also working with her husband on their empire and creating their own destiny. For more about the author go to www.VerleizLattimore.com and check out www.rennyconsulting.com.

www.ingramcontent.com/pod-product-compliance
Lightning Source LLC
Chambersburg PA
CBHW041531220426
43672CB00002B/3